Divorce is a Grown Up Problem

A book about divorce for young children and their parents

By Janet Sinberg

Illustrated by Nancy Gray

D1305345

AVON
PUBLISHERS OF BARD, CAMELOT AND DISCUS BOOKS

DIVORCE IS A GROWN UP PROBLEM is an original publication of Avon Books. This work has never before appeared in book form.

AVON BOOKS
A division of
The Hearst Corporation
959 Eighth Avenue
New York, New York 10019

First Avon Printing, March, 1978
Third Printing

AVON TRADEMARK REG. U.S. PAT. OFF. AND IN
OTHER COUNTRIES, MARCA REGISTRADA, HECHO EN
U.S.A.

Printed in the U.S.A.

Divorce is a Grown Up Problem

A book about divorce
for young children and their parents

by Janet Sinberg
Illustrated by Nancy Gray

JANET SINBERG obtained her Master's Degree in Child Development and Child Care from the University of Pittsburgh and has training in Play Therapy from the Pittsburgh Psychoanalytic Center. She has worked extensively with children and their families, and is currently a Play Therapist at the Western Pennsylvania School for Blind Children.

Janet is divorced and lives in Pittsburgh with her 3 sons, 3 hermit crabs, 1 cat, 1 ferret, and a goldfish.

NANCY GRAY is a graphic designer and illustrator of children's books. She recently received her degree in Fine Arts from Carnegie-Mellon University.

Nancy lives in Pittsburgh where she is a free lance artist.

For Aaron, Zachary, and Joshua.

Divorce is a Grown Up Problem

Preface for Parents

Making the decision to seek a divorce is an extremely difficult one. You already know that. When children are involved, most parents feel rather guilty. They wonder if the divorce will leave permanent scars, and often think it may be better to stay together "for the sake of the children." Most people who work with children feel that a home in which a divorce has taken place can be healthier than one in which a bad marriage continues to exist. Given care, understanding, emotional support, and love, children can weather such crises and grow to be happy, healthy, normal, and loving adults. But, the care, understanding, emotional support, and love must be there for them to continue to develop.

The purpose of this book is to help you and your child through a confusing, angry, and painful time. Just as you are experiencing a flood of anxious feelings, so is your child. You, however, have the words to define how you're feeling, and often the support of friends, family, or professional help. Often, young children don't have the words to describe how they feel about something painful. Instead, they may cry, regress, become angry, withdraw, feel guilty, and aren't able to describe what they are experiencing. This is a time when your child will need you to help him reorganize his life. You're probably trying very hard to do this for yourself. What you will find is that as your child can begin to understand your divorce and express his feelings about it, things should become easier for both of you.

This book has been designed to help a child understand what has happened to his family. It is a lap book, one to be read aloud by a parent, hopefully by both mother and father at different times. In this way you will be making yourself available to your child. It may open communication which will be valuable for both of you. This is a painful book, but as with all things that hurt, it helps to talk about them. It is also a hopeful book for a child, for it shows that although painful things do happen in life, it's not the end of the world.

Every family's circumstances and events are different. You may have more than one child, different custody arrangements, visitation rights, life styles, etc. Feel free to alter the text as much as you like as you read this. What is important is for you to be available to your child in order to help him through this time. He needs to talk, cry, feel angry, sad, and find his way through the confusion. And you can help. After all, that's what parents are for—helping.

Some Important Things for Divorcing Parents to Remember:

- Your child needs your support, understanding, and love.
- You needn't go into great detail about the specific reasons why you sought a divorce. These will have little meaning for your child and, in fact, may be frightening for him. Simple explanations will be easier to understand and be less threatening.
- Your child will need constant reassurance that you love him. He may believe that because you stopped loving your former spouse you might stop loving him. He needs to be told that this won't ever happen. You might say something about a parent's love being a special kind of love that never changes.
- Your child may demand extraordinary attention. While it's a time when he needs lots of extra support, it won't do him a great deal of good if he becomes the only focus of your life.
- When your child is with you, he may want to be with the missing parent. This will probably be painful for you. It might help to simply agree and tell him exactly when he'll see him or her: "You'll see Mommy tomorrow morning when she picks you up," or "Daddy will be here Friday afternoon to take you to his apartment."
- Your child may act quite infantile for a while. In times of stress or illness children often regress for a period of time as a way of backing up from something painful. This doesn't mean that he is a baby and won't ever grow up. He shouldn't be punished for this but rather supported to help him regain his former self-confidence.
- Your child should not be used as a weapon to get back at your former spouse. This is being unfair to the child. You are both adults, and while contacts with your ex may not be exactly cordial, it simply isn't fair to drag a child into your battles.
- When you are with your former spouse it won't help your child if he sees you arguing about who's going to get what when you divide property. These are issues you can deal with when he isn't around.
- Many times parents become overindulgent because they feel guilty about the divorce. Buying lots of new toys won't help the

way he is feeling. Love and understanding will do more good than three new dolls and a new set of blocks.

- It may be difficult for you to maintain discipline with your child. It's important, however, for you to continue to set limits as each of you did in the past. If he is out of control, he needs an adult to help him regain it.

- Your child needs to feel safe. He may become very anxious over even the smallest changes in his life for a while. Since he is having to deal with a major change, your divorce, little things may be very upsetting. He needs constant reassurance that you will keep him safe and secure.

- Your child may feel very angry about the divorce, but might find it difficult to let you know this. As a result, he may throw tantrums about many other things. It might help if you let him know that you understand that he's angry at his parents and that it's all right to feel this way. Anger is a normal reaction to a painful loss. He may need help in channeling his anger in a constructive fashion.

- Your child may feel guilty about the divorce, that somehow he was responsible for the separation by being bad or naughty. Some children who believe this may test their parents by constantly misbehaving in order to see if they will abandon them or stop loving them. It's important for you to tell your child, many times, that he was in no way responsible for your decision. It wasn't his fault.

- Your child may believe that he has the power to make his parents happy enough to want to get back together or even remarry. It's very important to remind him that the divorce wasn't his fault and that it isn't possible for him to patch things up between you. The divorce is final and he will have to accept that.

- Your child may feel strange or embarrassed about the divorce. Many children feel that theirs is the only family that has ever had such a thing happen. If you have friends or relatives who are divorced, it might help to point this out by saying something like, "You know Suzie's Mommy and Daddy are divorced, too, just like your Mommy and Daddy are."

- Your child is still a child. It won't help him or her to be told "Now you're the man of the house" or "You're Daddy's little woman now." A child needs to know that adults are still in charge of his world and will continue to be so.

- Some children may be afraid to go to bed or to sleep alone. Even though you may be lonely too, it's not the best idea for you to let him sleep with you. This will only confirm his fears that it really isn't safe to be alone. You can remind him that he has his own bed and so do you.

- Some of the things your child does may remind you of your former spouse, and make you feel angry. This is a normal reaction on your part. It's important, however, for your child to feel good about both of his parents and what he learns from each of them. It may be frightening for him to hear you say "You act just like your father (or mother) when you do that!" It might make him think that you could divorce him too.

- After a divorce, many parents feel that every bit of misbehavior or each period of unhappiness on their child's part is a direct result of the divorce. This simply isn't so. All children go through rough stages in their development and some periods are harder for them (and you) than others. You needn't go through the rest of your life thinking things would be easier or better for your child if only you hadn't gotten divorced.

- Your divorce is not the end of the world for you or your child. It's an unhappy and painful time for all of you, but your life will go on. With time, help, support, reassurance, and love, you and your child will continue to grow and develop.

Daddy doesn't live here anymore.
He used to live in our house with Mommy and me.
Now he lives in an apartment all by himself.

Mommy and I live here all by ourselves.

Mommy and Daddy got a divorce.
I don't even know what divorce means.
They spend a lot of time trying to explain it to me because I just don't understand.

Mommy said a long time ago she and Daddy
loved each other very much and they decided to get married.
But after they lived together for a long time, each one of them
had changed. They changed so much that they weren't happy
living together anymore.

Daddy said he and Mommy were unhappy living together.
They got mad at each other all the time.
Sometimes they yelled at each other and that was scary for me.
Sometimes they wouldn't even talk to each other.
That was even scarier.

That was when I started hearing that word — divorce.

Mommy told me "A divorce happens when a Mommy and Daddy can't ever be happy living together. It's a grown up problem, and it's not your fault. Sometimes they get mad and yell at each other. Sometimes they're so mad they won't even talk to each other. Sometimes they cry. This makes everyone in the family very sad. When a Mommy and Daddy are so unhappy living together, they get a divorce.
This means they won't live together anymore."

I wish my parents hadn't gotten divorced.
I wish they would just be happy again and we could all live together.
Mommy said this can't be. Daddy said they had tried and tried to be
happy together. But they just couldn't. So, they decided to get a divorce

This is how I feel about it:

Sometimes I feel really scared.
I worry about who's going to keep me safe.

Sometimes I feel so mad that I scream and cry.

Daddy says it's better to hit a pillow than it is to hit him.

Sometimes I feel sad and cry. I say I want to be alone,

but I really need people to help me.

Sometimes I think the divorce is my fault. I'm afraid the reason
Mommy and Daddy were unhappy is because I was bad.

This isn't so. Mommy said she and Daddy were unhappy because each one of them had changed so much.

The divorce wasn't my fault.

Sometimes I think I can make Mommy and Daddy get back together and be happy again if only I can be good enough.

Daddy said the divorce is his and Mommy's problem.
It wasn't my fault and I can't make them happy with each other.

Sometimes I think our family is different because my Daddy doesn't live with Mommy and me.

Mommy said lots of other kid's parents are divorced, too.

Sometimes I pretend it never happened.

But my parents are divorced,
and I think that's the way it will always be.

Sometimes I feel I have to be big and act more grown up.

But I don't feel so big. I'm still a little kid.

Sometimes when I'm with Mommy, I want my Daddy.
You see, I love my Daddy, too.

Sometimes when I'm with my Daddy, I want my Mommy.
That's because I love my Mommy, too.

A divorce is really a confusing thing.

Mommy and I still live in our house. It's different now that Daddy doesn't live here, but it's still our house. Mommy and I do lots of things together and she takes care of me when I'm with her. I've even started to go to school. Mommy will always be my Mommy.
She loves me and I love her.

Now that Daddy lives in his apartment, I can go and stay with him there. I have my own bed and sometimes I sleep there. I have toys to play with and books for Daddy to read to me. He takes care of me when I'm with him. Daddy will always be my Daddy. He loves me and I love him.

Mommy and Daddy seem happier now that they don't live together.
They don't get mad at each other so often. I can be happy with each
one of them even though they live in separate places.

Whenever I feel sad or angry about the divorce I talk with
Mommy or Daddy. It helps when I talk about it instead of just feeling it.
Mommy and Daddy love me and help me whenever they can.

I know that I love my Daddy and he loves me.

I guess divorce is a grown up problem,
the way my Mommy says it is.
It still makes a kid like me wonder about a lot of things.

I know that I love my Mommy and she loves me.

SUGGESTED READINGS ON DIVORCE
FOR PARENTS AND CHILDREN

Atkin, Edith and Rubin, Estelle, *PART-TIME FATHER* (New York: Vanguard Press, 1976.)

A sensitive and helpful book for men who are trying to redefine their roles as fathers—after the divorce. It provides great insight as it emphasizes the value of the divorced father's relationship with his child.

Despert, Louise, *CHILDREN OF DIVORCE* (Garden City, New York: Doubleday & Company, 1953.)

An excellent book for parents who are contemplating or are in the process of divorce. It focuses on the children and their needs during this period and provides practical advice on how parents can help to meet them.

Epstein, Joseph R. *DIVORCED IN AMERICA* (New York: E. P. Dutton & Company, 1974.)

A personal account of one man's experience of his divorce. It is a thoughtful book on the institution of divorce.

Fuller, Jan, SPACE: *THE SCRAPBOOK OF MY DIVORCE* (New York: Arthur Fields Books, Inc., 1973.)

An excerpt of a personal diary written by a young mother of her experience of divorce. She beautifully describes her pain and confusion during the trauma of the divorce, and goes on to tell of the reconstruction of her life as a woman and a mother.

Gardner, Richard A. *THE BOYS AND GIRLS BOOK ABOUT DIVORCE* (New York: Bantam Books, Inc., 1970.)

As the title implies, a book about divorce written for children (good readers and adolescents). Dr. Gardner explains the feelings a child may have about his parents' divorce and provides good advice on how to cope with them.

Gardner, Richard A. *THE PARENTS BOOK ABOUT DIVORCE* (Garden City, New York: Doubleday & Company, Inc., 1977.)

An excellent, comprehensive book for parents who are contemplating or have already completed divorce. He discusses how to explain divorce to children, the effects on children, and how to help children weather the crisis.

Grollman, Earl A., Ed. *EXPLAINING DIVORCE TO CHILDREN* (Boston: Beacon Press, 1969.)

A compilation of articles about divorce and children written by experts from different disciplines: psychiatry, sociology, law, psychology, and religion.

Grollman, Earl A., *TALKING ABOUT DIVORCE* (Boston: Beacon Press, 1975.)

A dialogue format book which is to be read aloud by parents and children—together. It explains why parents divorce and emphasizes the need for a child to understand and express his feelings about it.

Hirsch, Barbara B. *DIVORCE—WHAT A WOMAN NEEDS TO KNOW* (Chicago: Henry Regnery Company, 1973.)

A book by a practicing attorney which explores the legal aspects of divorce. It provides some concrete answers to questions about court procedures, property settlement, child custody, alimony, and tax matters.

Hunt, Morton, *THE WORLD OF THE FORMERLY MARRIED* (New York: McGraw-Hill, 1966.)

A look at the lives of those persons who have gone through divorce and how the experience has changed their lives.

Krantzler, Mel, *CREATIVE DIVORCE* (New York: The New American Library, 1973.)

A consideration of the emotional aspects of divorce—the pain, guilt, and confusion. The author takes the position that divorce can be a creative experience for the individual as it provides an opportunity for personal growth.

Mindey, Carol, *THE DIVORCED MOTHER* (New York: McGraw-Hill, 1969.)

A book for the divorcee with children. The author provides practical advice on how to cope with the multitude of problems—social, economic, and personal—a divorced mother faces as she reconstructs her life and those of her children.

Sheresky, Norman and Mannes, Marya, *UNCOUPLING—THE ART OF COMING APART* (New York: The Viking Press, 1972.)

A legal and psychological guide for those contemplating divorce. The authors provide a look at the legal maze of divorce proceedings, and proffer advice on how to avoid some of the pitfalls of the system.